AF198657

Why

(... I write)

Klaus Ebner

Why
(... I write)

The German National Library catalogs this publication in the
German National Bibliography. The detailed Cataloging-in-
Publication Data is available from http://dnb.dnb.de

Library of Congress Name Authority File no2011078268

Cover design: Klaus Ebner, using a picture by Janet Gooch
on Pixabay, www.pixabay.com, and a photograph
by Karl Grabherr, www.grabherr-photography.com
Published by BoD–Books on Demand, Norderstedt, FRG
Printed in the European Union
ISBN: 978-3-751903790

Table of Content

I wish to express my thanks to my American friend Anne Armstrong Holcomb who read the book from cover to cover, improving the language.

The Question

At least once in a lifetime, every writer asks *why* he or she writes. I came across such an assertion several times; in articles and commentaries, and certainly also in philological textbooks. But is that really so?

I believe the truth is slightly different: It isn't the writers themselves who come up with such a question, maybe based on some inner necessity; no, not at all—this question is brought up by others, by the social environment, by readers, friends and family, by journalists and the scholars of literature departments at universities who are keen on finding out the trigger or the source of inspiration which can suddenly turn otherwise respectable citizens into authors.

The question of the *why* seems to require a justification. But a justification for what? It almost seems that writers should be seen as aberrations within society, as *outlaws*, as irresponsible daydreamers and madmen. Well, maybe we are a little bit crazy, because pursuing a vocation, which in most cases requires a lot of work but does not bring in much money (and guarantees a living to only a choice few), has in fact very little to do with economic thinking or even with reason.

To be honest, I never asked myself the question of *why* I write. Writing is part of my self-worth. It is the expression of my personality and I can hardly imagine living without it, as I cannot imagine living without one of my limbs. On the other hand, I've often been asked the question, and in most cases I looked up with an open mouth (ergo stupidly) and didn't know what to answer. I probably didn't even understand *what* was actually being asked, but eventually the question maneuvered me into a long process of reflection.

The question of *why* is not a simple one. In order to get closer to it and ultimately find something like a viable answer, it seems to me advisable to explore the how and why of key developments in my childhood that gradually shaped me into who I am today.

The Beginning

Of course, everything starts with childhood. The question of why in this context doesn't really apply, because much of what happens during childhood is not subject to willful control, and therefore several things will remain a mystery forever.

My strong affinity for language revealed itself early on. My mother has repeatedly said that at the *age of one* I spoke fluently and in full sentences. I find it difficult to take this statement at face value, probably because I don't know a single child (including my own) who had such a striking language competence at only one year of age.

What I remember clearly is that anything like dialect or slang was completely absent during the first years of my life. We lived in the city of Vienna, and it was important to my parents that their son speak *beautifully*, which meant: according to *written German*, often and incorrectly called *High German*. (My family was not aware that the entirety of all Upper and Central German language varieties, registers and dialects belong to High German, and only Low German in the far north of the Federal

Republic of Germany strays off course.) In my family, I seldom heard anyone using the Viennese slang (which is no longer a real dialect from a linguistic point of view); most of my exposure to dialect came about during our family vacations in Carinthia (especially at Lake Klopein); my kindergarten attendance was limited to a few barely significant weeks.

One day when I was four or five, my mother hurtled towards me in the stairwell (I forgot why we stood there) and accused me of having uttered a *really bad word*. I had no idea what she was talking about. We blundered into a discussion full of reproach, objection, and curiosity. Since I didn't know the reason for her anger, I urged her to tell me what the word was, because only then would I be able to tell her whether it had actually come out of my mouth or not. This discussion felt like half an hour (it probably lasted only ten minutes or so) before she finally came out with the *bad word* (of which I now unfortunately have no remembrance at all). At this point, I heard it for the first time in my life; I don't know whether it was obscene, but I am sure that it was a dialect word.

The Viennese slang found its way into my personal language in high school, but it showed up only when I was alone with classmates or friends. This was because I never felt slang or dialect to be my own language, but instead something alien that I was forced to use even though I loathed it and wanted to reject it. The fact that I was allowed and even obliged to speak to the teachers *according to written German*, was a ray of hope, which I appreciated immensely. (That said, the two teachers who strongly advocated speaking slang with the students in order to have good rapport with them, were ticked off with me from the get-go, and they retaliated with poor grades.)

While I attended lower secondary school, nobody could have foreseen that I would develop a great affection for foreign languages. I'll never forget my first major test in English (a subject that I apparently considered to be beneath my dignity in the first year of junior high school), when I stumbled over the question: *Does your friend speak German?* In spite of my constant inattentiveness, I had noticed during the lessons that personal names are capitalized in English, and so I scribbled my answer intrepidly into the test book: *Yes, German is my friend.*

From the age of twelve on, I had Latin. A six-year fiasco! The reason I never failed completely was because of my Latin teacher, who apparently sensed my talents (which didn't include Latin, by the way) and then somehow dragged me through all those years.

But two years later, during the school vacation, I discovered French. How should I say: it was love at first sight! In the first year of study I left my classmates far behind, and then I started to learn other Romance languages on my own. It was (and is still) an exorbitant delight to learn these languages and to sample others as well. And, every language drew me to its literature, to novels and stories from other cultures, and on to poetry and theater. I wondered about the slightly different usage of literary terms, and I quickly became able to list the names of writers whom my comrades had never heard of.

The Books (I)

As I said, slang and dialect are not a part of my literary skill set. But the Austrian variant of standard German and the style of written language are. I started reading books early on during elementary school, as soon as I had acquired enough proficiency to manage it, which was also due in large part to my mother's influence. I remember a young adult series in which all the books had a dark red spine. This series featured literary classics, some of which had been written for kids, while others represented great works of world literature that had been abbreviated to the needs of children, with simplified language. There was *Treasure Island* as well as *The Adventures of Tom Sawyer*, *Moby Dick* and *Gulliver's Travels*. Only years later did I notice that I had been ingesting (without any ulterior motives) primarily translations of English-language literature. The series of books might also have contained *Twenty Thousand Leagues Under the Sea* or *The Adventures of Pinocchio*, but I no longer recall this exact detail. On the other hand, one book did stick in my mind; it was about an Indian boy who, probably in the 17th or 18th century, lives in the forests of the Appalachian Mountains, gets lost as a result of a test of courage and struggles with growing up. I think it was not a well-known work of literature, because its title disappeared in the fog of my past childhood without leaving a trace.

Before each Christmas I created lists on which I meticulously determined who in the family should gift me which book. I knew that in the case of my great aunt, I had to search through the (quite limited) catalog of a book club, while the other family members were easier to handle. Usually it worked out fine— my parents made sure that my book requests were fulfilled. Just before my tenth birthday, I asked for Franz Werfel's *The Forty Days of Musa Dagh*. Probably the colorful cover picture appealed to me, because it was several decades before I finally read this novel. During junior high, I built a collection of Karl May books, which I considered awfully famous, although I read exclusively only the volumes that were set in North or South America; when I learned from a television show that May is almost unknown outside of German-speaking countries, I was shocked. My Christmas wish lists included non-fiction books and the first classics of world literature. When I was about fifteen, I discovered Anglo-American science fiction, together with my school friend Peter, and devoured a number of English language books. I was already buying them for myself (luckily, SF paperbacks were cheap). Eventually, I developed the desire to write science fiction stories by myself, and I inflicted them upon my English and French teachers; they had to correct my pages of writing, which were packed with mind-blowing, outrageous stories, (and correct them they did, thoroughly—a late thank you for that!).

I don't remember at what point I turned to more literary works. However, I do remember well my first reading of Kafka's novel, *The Trial*: I understood almost nothing and felt tormented by a boring text in which I didn't even know what I had read just two pages before. Today, I smile about it and shake my head, since I consider Kafka's *Trial* one of the greatest works of world literature.

And it was world literature of which I was very fond at my school leaving examination in German. Since my reading list was so full of foreign-language books (translated to German, of course), my teacher asked me to thin it out and please include a little bit more of Goethe-Schiller-Stifter-Schnitzler. I gave in reluctantly. (And then I was disappointed that she didn't ask me a single question about what I thought was the greatest in world literature.)

In my senior year I wanted a recently published boxed set with the complete works of Paul Celan as a Christmas gift from my parents. I was terribly disappointed when I didn't find it under the tree, but I bravely kept my mouth shut. Only when my mother took me aside, revealed to me that the delivery from the publisher had taken too long, and handed me a voucher, was the evening saved (and I secretly felt ashamed of my whiny reaction). After the holidays I cheerfully tramped to the bookshop (it no longer exists) near Saint Stephen's Cathedral in Vienna's center, in order to take possession of my new treasure.

The Pioneers

It might be that I forgot to mention this aspect of why I write: several writers have published notes, essays or entire books on the subject. It is obvious that a writing person is keen on becoming familiar with these sorts of texts. Therefore—and that is what I meant by having forgotten—the question of why write was brought up to me from literature itself. During my philological studies, I have repeatedly come across such statements.

Jean-Paul Sartre was one of the first to bring up the question of why write. He was an author and philosopher whose writings I liked when I was still a student. I read his plays and novels from start to finish, and I started to dig into Sartre's philosophy and his autobiographical writings. Then I got my hands on the thin booklet *Qu'est-ce que la littérature ?* I devoured this essay, not so much as a student but as a future writer (and read it a second time several years later). In keeping with his perception of existentialism, Sartre maintains the thesis that literature could not exist without a (political) commitment, or that it if it did, it would be worthless. He shows examples and demonstrates the implicit political or social motivation behind many contemporary texts, while simultaneously attacking those authors who are more dedicated to art itself, whose approach comes from symbolism or who worship the idea of *l'art pour l'art*. According to Sartre, literature is always written for other people, and therefore the focus on art itself makes no sense at all.

Sartre's essay impressed me, there is no doubt about that. It flattered my youthful ideas, and when I read through my publications in literary magazines of the time (which, nowadays, seem to me embarrassing), it is clear that I had also tried to make some sociopolitical contribution, which translated to a literary motivation. Nevertheless, reading Sartre's book also caused a feeling of dissatisfaction and consternation, because I didn't appreciate the fact that the author sentenced and condemned a whole lot of writers—some of whom I admired. Over the years, I became more and more convinced that Sartre's (in French:) *engagement* represent *one* motivation to write, but by no means the only one, and, above all, not a mandatory one.

In her book *How to write*, Gertrude Stein skipped one step and didn't even ask herself why someone would or should write. She accepts it as a fact without commenting on it, and she concentrates directly on writing techniques and the linguistic skills that writers should develop and internalize in order to produce valuable literature.

George Orwell spent his (short) life dealing with political and ideological language. His motivation to write was a political commitment—in the spirit of Sartre—and the question of why he chose this line is answered succinctly in the short essay *Why I write* with his personal experiences as a young man in the British colonies (as a policeman in Burma), and shortly thereafter in the Spanish Civil War. The explanation of the Catalan writer Montserrat Roig (who also died much too young) is similar: she attributed her impulse to write to the oppression to which the Catalan population was brutally exposed under Franco's regime. Her compatriot Josep Pla, who created a magnificent literary work under the same dictatorship, probably felt a similar drive.

In the essay *Why write?*, Paul Auster claims that he got into writing more or less by accident, simply because he got used to carrying a pencil with him after failing to get an autograph from the baseball star he admired when he was eight years old because he didn't have a pen or pencil with him. And at some point, he states, if you have a pencil, you eventually use it—and that's how he became a writer.

As one can recognize easily, many of my writing colleagues identify a distinct reason why they write; some, like Jean-Paul Sartre, are smart enough to describe the theoretical foundation, and: to justify their work.

Nevertheless, I have my doubts. I can hardly imagine that someone would be capable of creating literature if the ability or disposition to do this had not been in the future writer's personality from the very beginning. The start of the literary writing process may occur early on or considerably later, but I don't believe in entirely external motivations or roots.

The School

Does school affect the development of a writer? I think you can see it either way. Of course, we learn to read and write at school. We get acquainted with books and literature (at least during the 1970s and 1980s it was so), and we are encouraged to interpret short stories and poems. (Poetry interpretation can be compared easily with today's food industry: first of all, everything is broken down to the smallest parts, and then you reassemble them following a totally new recipe.) German classes (or language classes in general) certainly leave their mark, and the teachers can encourage and nurture a linguistic and narrative talent or, on the other hand, shut it down. I can say with a clear conscience that my professors belonged to the facilitators, although I don't know to what extent they were aware of this.

But let me start at the beginning: My remembrance of elementary school is astonishingly vague, and I had to believe my mother when she told me that my elementary school teacher had placed great value on proficiency in the German language and on correct spelling among her pupils.

It must have been during the fourth grade of elementary school that I found a bunch of scratch-off pictures, presumably in chewing gum paper or among wrappers from other sweets, that I could paste into school booklets, on sheets (and probably also onto other objects). I scrounged a three-column vocabulary book from my mother, which eventually became my personal secret journal. On each page, I wrote a short story, in the evening and sometimes already in bed, and glued some issue-related scratch-off pictures between the written lines. The stories were about pirates and Chinese people, about adventures on the sea and battles against the monsters, which at that time I thought would live in the ocean. If one of the stories grew too long, I used a double page; it had to be a left and a right page, because I hated turning the page in the middle of the story. I wrote everything neatly in ink and in what we call *the brownie script* in my country—a print-script—because I wished that posterity would one day be able to decipher my dreadful cursive. When I made a mistake and had to overwrite or delete a word, I became hopping mad, because at that age I had already developed a certain sensitivity for aesthetics. I so wanted to create a *really beautiful storybook.*

Much to my deep regret this childlike writing attempt did not survive.

I stumbled across the next milestone—if it was one—during the second year of middle school. I decided I had to write a theater play, then rehearse it with my classmates and finally perform it at school. A German teacher (i.e. not mine!) agreed to supervise our rehearsals in the afternoon. Officially this meant he was to support us, but it resulted him napping regularly and snoring loudly. We bought crepe paper, glue and colored cardboard because we had to create Roman and Gallic costumes with very few resources. My play was about the invincible Gauls in Aremorica—a quite cheap copy of an Asterix comic, the basic idea of which I wanted to bring to the stage. The first disappointment came when I finally finished the play and brought it to the class: it was only three pages long; typed on A4 sheets and single-spaced, but only three pages, which were probably performed within twenty minutes at most. My classmates rolled their eyes and bluntly expressed their scorn. The whole thing fizzled out, and the teacher didn't want to continue staying at school in the afternoon (maybe we had been too noisy for his well-deserved sleep). I was exceedingly sorry, but frankly it was dumb luck that my blundering didn't develop into an even bigger disaster.

In the fourth year of junior high school, a new and still very young German teacher was hired.

The Teacher

She had recently passed her teacher's exam and had just started her career at our high school as a professor of German and eventually mathematics: Christine Hollmann. As one expects from young teachers, she was very committed and motivated. I think we were her first class, and that's how she encountered: me.

Although bad behavior had never been my style, during the first weeks and months of her German class, I was insolent, cheeky, and extremely arrogant.

I did not listen to her, ignored her openly, didn't give any answers or, at best, had my comrades deliver them on small pieces of paper. Maybe I felt superior to the supposedly weak teacher; maybe I wanted, at least once in my time as a student, to be the *asshole of my class*—frankly, I have not the slightest clue what demon haunted me those days.

However, Mrs. Hollmann persevered. She tried to counter with objectivity, hiding her anger from me and probably also her despair. She praised the linguistic quality of my punitive essays, although I tortured her regularly with the word count.

And then she did something, maybe weeks late, but in the end still in time, which was the only right thing to do in this situation: she summoned my mother! And I feared nothing more than her (something the teacher could not have known yet).

I remember well the day my mother showed up to meet her for a parent-teacher conference before class. We had Hollmann during the last period of the day, so it was she who released us finally from the dressing room when we had gathered our things. My stomach felt weak, and so I approached her and asked her despondently about my mother's reaction. But instead of answering me, she was flabbergasted (I think she almost embraced me) and burst out: "Dear Klaus, you are finally talking to me!"

From this moment on, my strange lunacy was history. Within a very short time I was at a loss to explain this miserable kick-off. But since our teacher had the reputation at this secondary school of being very strict, I had to grapple for a long time with the irksome feeling that my bad behavior might have actually screwed her up. (Today I know that she has retained her commitment and her open character.)

Why am I mentioning all this? I owe this teacher thanks for five years of excellent lessons in my native language, German. Nevertheless, I wasn't always attentive, and I remember numerous times during my German studies at university where I thought: "Gosh, I've heard that already from my German teacher!" She made language history accessible to us and gave a small introduction to Middle High German; I was able to revel in the literature I loved and allowed to choose the topics of my presentations quite freely.

It was this German teacher who pointed my school friend Peter and me toward the literary competition *Young Literature from Austria*, which was sponsored by the Austrian federal publisher Bundesverlag. It was probably her intention that the class participate in voting for the submitted stories (because with some luck, school classes could win a small remuneration), but for Peter and me it was as a matter of course from the very first day that we would submit our own writings.

We were seventeen, and until then we had produced only a few science fiction stories overflowing with exaggeration and some bizarre anecdotes in our homework and language exams. I no longer recall the details of these events, but I believe that this moment, our lift-off to the writing competition the German teacher had steered us toward, triggered a wholehearted and permanent commitment to the creative writing process. Of course, I still had a lot to learn and a long way to go (about which I had no idea at that time), and the youth prize for a novella, which I was awarded by the Austrian bank Erste Österreichische Spar-Casse, mainly through the advocacy of critic and jury member Hans Weigel, shortly after my school leaving exams, must be seen at best as a tiny, stumbling step in the direction of my career as an author, which, of course, I didn't realize at the time.

The Books (II)

Originally, I wanted to become an interpreter. I switched to translation studies after having realized that I wasn't even able simply to repeat a text that was spoken on the radio—quite a bad deficit for simultaneous interpreting. My talents have always been in writing. In the second year of university, I started studying English and Romance Languages in addition, but I soon gave up English, chose French as my major and enrolled in German for my minor. I took on these additional studies because the interpreting department has absolutely nothing to do with literature. The people there translate specialized texts, business, legal and technological papers, then maybe some articles from the humanities, which also include literary studies. But nobody translates literary works there.

In the Romance and German departments, I officially had the right to deal with literature on a regular basis. I continued to grow my personal library—this time adding French literature—and even wrote my own texts.

While the existentialist writers receded slowly into the background, I got to know the school of the *Nouveau Roman* and to appreciate in particular the books of Alain Robbe-Grillet. I discovered André Gide and was enraptured by his early novel *Paludes*; I was introduced to Gide's diaries by the professors of the Romance department and found the late work *Thésée* to be a linguistic pearl. Nathalie Sarraute's prose, however, seemed bulky and unpalatable to me, and it took years before I could get anything out of her finely carved style of writing.

There are so many names that I can hardly think of them all. Anyway, I suspect that French literature influenced me most in my writing.

It was my second language that served as an entrance to Italian literature: Cesare Pavese and the linguistically complex novels by Carlo Emilio Gadda. However, it was Italo Calvino who became my favorite; a lecture at the Romance department drew my attention to the great book (consisting of nothing but the beginnings of several novels) *Se una notte d'inverno un viaggiatore*, and I like to browse the scientifically bizarre short stories of the *Cosmicomiche* still today.

The Club

Our literary club was founded without my intervention, but Peter made sure that I could be a steering member almost from the beginning. We were a bunch of young people who not only wrote literature but also wanted to publish their works. The association edited the literary magazine TEXTE (yep, in upper case): pages and text blocks typed on the typewriter and pasted onto a template sheet, after which it was all copied and stapled a few hundred times. Everything was manual, of course. The few books and brochures that we published by ourselves shortly thereafter were also produced manually.

Today, most of the texts published this way seem rather embarrassing to me: linguistically unpolished, full of mistakes, and sometimes even the story itself is ridiculous. The fact that we had to deliver mandatory copies of each publication to Austria's National Library must be blamed for the fact that we can never undo this amateur tinkering.

In addition to the published short stories and poems from this time (which cannot compare at all with the poetry I write today), I also authored novels and plays. I finished four novels in total. Fortunately, there is nothing left from this time, but it showed me clearly what it means to plan, work out, and complete a large piece of prose like a novel. With these works I proved to myself that I *can* do it (whereas the dramas were more drama-laden and proved that I *could not* do it).

We all worked with commitment. (Sartre would have loved it.) We wrote eagerly against war, in favor of equal rights for women, against violence and in favor of environmental protection (which was still in its infancy at that time). We really believed we would be able to improve the world with our literature, and we basked in something between naivety and arrogance. Well, it *could* actually have turned into something!

At last, I started to write a new novel. But then, 1987 happened—the year in which all my plans, intentions, and dreams ground to a halt.

The Interruption

The year 1987 brought some radical changes. I completed my final semesters at the university and so I started working as a freelance translator (curiously I rarely translated from my main languages, French and Italian, but rather from Portuguese and English). Our literary club showed signs of disbanding as my associate colleagues reoriented themselves into completely different professions. I purchased my first computer (a PC with an 8088 processor and a 20 MB [!] hard drive, which, at the time, I seriously thought totally oversized) because I realized that in order to be capable of offering professional translation services, I would need a word processor. However, the most important turning point was the birth of my first child.

Suddenly obliged to guarantee a family's livelihood and acutely aware that my annual writer's income wouldn't even suffice for one week, I looked for other opportunities. I published a book about the word processor I knew so well, and I started teaching this software in a training center. My role as a father especially was new and initially quite time-consuming, and it was: the literature that fell by the wayside.

My writing had come to an end. That's what I thought. The words *for now* crept into my mind repeatedly, but I tried to ignore them. After 1987 I didn't write a thing. That's what I believed, too. With hindsight, it looks different. Admittedly, there were no more tales, no short stories, and of course I didn't write a new novel. We quietly buried our literary club and I lost the few contacts I had. But what remained that could never be eradicated was the faint feeling that I would still be a writer!

An initial misconception on my part was an activity that I now regard as a kind of substitute act. I wrote IT books and specialized articles for IT magazines in Austria, Germany and—in English—the United Kingdom. Books on word processing, spreadsheets and the brand-new desktop publishing. This all has nothing to do with a writer's profession, i.e. literary writing. Or has it? Well, for five years I didn't do anything literary and I really suffered because of it. My non-fiction texts ran on a separate track, and I never saw them in the context of literature. Many years later I began to understand that this activity had indeed strengthened and sharpened my writing skills. (If you have to discuss an integrated office package over exactly fifteen lines within one narrow newspaper column, you automatically learn to master the language and to never again accept it the other way round.)

Several times I attempted to resume writing stories, and I even played with the idea of writing weird tales which would take place in an IT environment, in order to offer them to a publisher of computer books. However, nothing came out of it and the paper remained as empty as my brain. I only wrote down a few diary notes on small pieces of paper that I would consolidate years later.

In 1992 my son was five years old. The fall of the Berlin Wall lay behind us, and I made my living as a software instructor. One particular day, I had worked late into the night, probably preparing a new curriculum. Shortly before midnight I shut down the PC and went to the bathroom. Somehow, I felt strange; a feeling of alleviation seemed to take hold of me. I thought of flying and the air that would rush through my fingers. After brushing my teeth, my heart started pounding; I went to bed anyway. And then I saw it clearly in front of me: the jump, the ascent into the air, the Eiffel Tower below me, I felt the sun's rays on my cheek and how the mild air slid over my hands and passed between my fingers.

Feverishly and yet quietly (not wanting to wake the family) I jumped up, and in the living room I scribbled an entire page at an incredible pace. Back in bed, I lay awake for hours. The next day I chained myself to the computer and typed a short, multi-page story without stopping. A system crash (without having backed up the brand-new data) put me on the verge of a nervous breakdown, since I had to restart from scratch.

With an inner excitement I had never experienced before, the story *Höhenflug* (*Altitude Flight*) came into being, as well as the vow to never again abandon literature.

The Books (III)

And once again the books. They accompany me from year to year, from decade to decade. But the type of books I read is changing. This has to do not only with my advancing age, but also with what interests me at a specific point due to private or professional causes. At the beginning of the 2000s, specifically in 2001 and 2002, the company for which I work to earn my daily living, gave me the marvelous opportunity to attend the technical conferences of Microsoft, which, in both years, took place in Barcelona.

I had started to learn Catalan when I was seventeen. During my studies of Romance languages, I had always been interested in the Catalan culture, which at the time represented a very marginal topic at the university of Vienna. Although I chose a subject related to Catalonia for my diploma thesis, I had to write my paper in French.

Following the IT speeches and workshops, I had time to roam the Catalan capital and invade various bookstores, which to my delight stayed open much longer than they did in Austria (until nine or ten was quite common in Catalonia and Spain, while in my own country they closed at six o'clock). My language skills at this time were at a rather rudimentary level despite the efforts of my friend Joan, the Catalan schoolteacher, who had provided me for years with a bulk of information and learning material from the *Principat*. As I returned from the Barcelona conferences, I carried a total of about fifty books in my suitcase—current Catalan literature and also some non-fiction books on political, cultural and legal issues.

This alone doesn't mean a lot; at best it reveals that the open space on my bookshelves shrank again noticeably.

But within two and a half years I *read* all these books, more than seven thousand pages in total. This reading experience, which I had not initially planned, not only laid the foundation for solid linguistic skills, but also for writing poetry in the Catalan language, which started spontaneously shortly afterwards.

My library continued to grow. In one of my novels, the main character humorously calls his treasured books his first, second and third library. I've not done that in *my own* life, but it would in fact be appropriate.

The Catalans

It happened at night. (Of course, the night was dark—every night is dark!) I had just gone to bed, but I could not sleep, and various words and sentence fragments haunted me—Catalan sentences.

I switched on the lamp again, drew a slip of paper from the desk and, with a pencil, scrawled down the snippets that were floating in my brain. And then another one. And then one more.

How should I say: I looked at the lines on my sheet and the lines looked at me. And after we had been eyeing each other for a while, I mumbled: "Oh my, that's a poem ..."

In the following days, I wrote many more of them. Of course, I knew that the intense reading of Catalan literature over the past months had developed a life of its own in my head. Individual words and phrases that I had read somewhere melted into something new about which I didn't yet know what to think. I decided to collect everything together and take notes. A few weeks later I had a word processor file with more than one hundred pages. Separated into three sections, they contained different types of poetry. In the first section, the poems were very short and almost resembled haikus; in the second, several stories and events were told; and the third section collected various views of the three cities that in a certain way define my life: Vienna, Paris and Barcelona.

Still undecided what to do with this volume, I decided to ask someone for advice. I contacted my Catalan friend Josep, a renowned writer, and asked him for his opinion. I bluntly said that if he thought this poetry was crap, he should just tell me without mincing words.

But he made no such response. On the contrary. To my surprise, he liked these poems, particularly the short ones as he told me, none of which had titles. The corrections he made in my file were even more astonishing, because he found surprisingly little to complain about in my verses. In about a quarter of the poems he had marked several mistakes—sometimes wrong spellings, sometimes an incorrect word or an incomprehensible phrasing—but the rest had remained untouched.

From these very first poems not much survived. A few of them found their way into my first book of poetry in a modified form, but I purged everything else. Josep (known in the Catalan Countries as J.N. Santaeulàlia) wrote a foreword to my debut with Catalan poetry, *Vermells* (*Shades of Red*). I succeeded in publishing the volume in Catalonia, as a bilingual edition, since I had included a German translation. (The original idea for this translation was that it would enable me to sell the book also in German speaking countries. I was however amazed to discover how difficult it is even to translate the poetry I myself wrote into my own native language!)

Without the subsequent reactions of the Catalan people, my book would have remained a solitary and maybe insolent experiment. But I caused a little uproar with my publication. I had initiated the contact with the daily newspaper AVUI myself, and the editor-in-chief immediately asked one of his employees to write an article about me. After a short email exchange in which I tried to give answers to her questions as precisely as possible (and of course, there was "*why* I would write in Catalan"), her article appeared in the cultural section of the newspaper and literally knocked my socks off: it was an entire large-format page including a giant photo of me (which in turn nourished my suspicion that she really didn't want to write much). One day later, the editorial staff of the Catalan radio, *Catalunya Ràdio*, suddenly contacted me. By phone. They said they had already tried to reach me via different means (in fact my publisher confirmed so shortly afterwards), and they wanted to have an interview with me on a popular talk show during their early evening program. Live and on the same day. I still remember how nervous I was, but the moderator of the show had everything under control. He spoke in a way (i.e., a bit slowly and clearly) that let me understand every word without any problem, and so I was able to answer his questions accordingly. (After the interview, I confessed to the editorial staff in an email how much I had trembled with nervousness and that I now wanted to change my completely sweat-soaked t-shirt.) An online newspaper soon published a review of my book, written by a poet friend of mine, Marta Pérez i Sierra, and several months later I found out by accident that there is an article about me in the country's prestigious *Enciclopèdia Catalana*.

At least *one* important reason for writing is the motivation, which was stimulated enormously by the Catalans' encouragement for my Catalan book.

I didn't see any reason for stopping, and so I wrote additional books of poetry. Of course, I still remained suspicious with regard to the linguistic and literary quality of my poems. Why? This is simply explained: I was aware that many Catalans feel flattered because, as a non-Catalan person without any family ties to that country, I write my poems in Catalan, thus in a language that is under strong political pressure, and, in addition, mostly unknown in an international context. I feared that they might praise and esteem my poetry for that reason only. But some years later, in 2014, I was awarded a Catalan poetry prize (*Premi de Poesia Parc Taulí*) for another manuscript and thus I established myself against all native speakers in this competition. From then on, there was no excuse left, and I accepted the logic that if my poems were not good enough, the Catalans wouldn't have given me a literary award.

The answer to the question of *why* I write Catalan poetry seems sophisticated and, above all, not very straightforward. What came about more or less by chance, based on my reading habits, received such a boost from the enthusiastic reaction of the Catalans, that this rather uncommon genre for an Austrian forms an integral part of my literature. As a matter of fact, I can even say that Catalan poems are much easier to compose for me than German ones. This may seem unusual, and in fact, it is. But maybe it is true, as Samuel Beckett once put it, in his similar, bilingual situation: that I move more freely, more informally and, in a certain way, more courageously in my foreign language.

The Why

The question of why. Does it work at all? I mean, it sounds like a banal cop out if I simply respond: because I must. And it was precisely this banality, this triteness that people accused me of when I actually answered the question in this way.

It may be that this I-write-because-I-must convention *is* trite. On the other hand, is that not also an indication that many writers really see it that way?

The compulsion to write, the inability to let it drop, the feeling of being driven to write runs like a golden thread through the history of literature. Franz Kafka once compared it to a terminal illness.

Writers may at times struggle with writer's block (which is also commonplace in the literary world), but they do not think of stopping writing. And even if they consider ending their career as a writer and act on that decision, they will quickly realize that they, like me, are incapable of doing it. Whoever writes cannot easily stop doing so. People who write may be able to do many things, but one thing they cannot do is: stop writing. (And when I learn about someone who was in fact able to abandon the writing profession, I profoundly doubt that this person had ever been serious about it.)

The evolution of a writer doesn't follow fixed rules. The approaches, the creative processes and what is commonly known as inspiration are utterly different. Investigating the motivation of writers either leads to a new discovery each time or is completely ineffective because the evidence is insufficient.

I've *never* considered carrying a booklet (or notepad) and a pen as a rule. In addition, I think it is exaggerated to think that their presence alone would suffice to trigger a literary writing process. Many ideas that I have come up when there is absolutely no way to write them down: when I'm standing naked and wet in the shower, traveling without any writing facilities, attending a very important company meeting. These ideas often disappear instantly, which makes me sad (and grouchy), and they will come back to me only on quite rare occasions. Maybe this procedure is due to my memory, which I think is *not always* reliable; however, perhaps it makes sense because the ideas that disappear and never return to me could possibly, upon closer examination, turn out to be worthless and thus negligible.

Basically, I don't like this *why*. It feels tenacious, sticky, and distasteful. For whatever reason the why arises as a question, lies beyond my knowledge and probably also beyond my comprehension. But it also seems clear to me that this question will not stop pursuing me, and it will track me down wherever I try to hide. The question of why is an unloved companion that forces me to deal with it. Forever.

Well then?

I write because it is the way I express myself. I write because it corresponds to my self-image as a person and as a member of our society. I write because it has to be so. I write because the earth turns around the sun, the planets do the same, our central star moves around the hub of the Milky Way, because the number and the dimensions of the celestial bodies exceed by far our mental capacities and we know so frighteningly little about these things.

I write because I am.

Klaus Ebner was born in 1964 in Vienna, Austria. Today he lives in Schwechat, Lower Austria, with his family. During the 1980ies he studied Romance languages and German philology. He writes short prose, stories, novels and essays, as well as poetry in German and Catalan.

He was awarded the Wiener Werkstattpreis in 2007, the Second Short Story Prize of the Austrian Writers' Association in 2010 and the Catalan poetry prize Premi de Poesia Parc Taulí in 2014.

Also available:
»Andorra«, photo essay, iBooks 2012
Several German and Catalan books

www.klausebner.eu